FINISHING LINE PRESS

www.finishinglinepress.com

La Revedere
(Goodbye)

poems by

Adela Sinclair

Finishing Line Press
Georgetown, Kentucky

La Revedere
(Goodbye)

ACKNOWLEDGMENTS

Grateful to the editors of the following publications, in which versions of
some of these poems first appeared:

Olney Magazine: "Topogan (Bloody Slide)"
                "Plate"
                "Garden"

Other Worldly Women Press: "On April 28, 1986, Chernobyl Exploded"

The Journal of Latina Critical Feminism: "La Revedere"

Publisher: Leah Huete de Maines
Editor: Christen Kincaid
Cover Art: Tony Vita
Author Photo: Piaskowski

Order online: www.finishinglinepress.com
            also available on amazon.com

Author inquiries and mail orders:
Finishing Line Press
PO Box 1626
Georgetown, Kentucky 40324
USA

Table of Contents

This book is dedicated to my family

La revedere

La revedere room.
La revedere house.
La revedere green gate, no 94.
Strada Clujului.
La revedere place where I slid off my bike.
Your voice slid down my shoulder.
I wanted to catch the wind.
I swallowed a fly.

La revedere airplane flying low above our house
that shakes everything in cupboards:
cups, plates, knives and forks.
La revedere Buni.
La revedere Dedi.

I took the bicycle and rode it
on the cobblestone street to *Alimentara*.
Nothing was on the shelves
of the grocery store.
I wanted candy.
Mama wanted butter.
Tata wanted cigarettes.
Buni wanted sugar.
Dedi wanted bread.
Leftover bread from yesterday's batch
slid out of my hands
onto the kitchen table.

The train choo-chooed farewell as it left the station.
La revedere Arad.
*La revedere Alina, Mihaela, Florin, Cristina, Simona, Melania and
Lucky.*
La revedere Dedi.
La revedere Buni.
I passed the neighbor's house on the way to school.
A boy pushed me off my bike.

I spit and got him!
La revedere.

Stoop where the neighbor sat and chewed
day old bread, making more saliva
to soften the crust.

La revedere garden where I sat and drew a flower in the grass.
The grapes were not ripe.

Goodbye on October 25, 1987.
The day I sat on Pan-Am
I flew over our house.
Buni and *Dedi* heard my roars.
The house shook.
The last *La revedere.*

Paper Children

They never imagined
what they would do to children.
But they were once innocent
and the masquerade continued
into young adulthood.
We were their first experiment.
Their first puppeteering job.
Playing us like accordions.
Who remembers the paper children
we once were?

I've crushed fresh mint leaves
between my teeth.
I've renounced the "master
and servant."
Who is the one who possesses?
I've renounced my memory,
my most recalcitrant obsession.
I am a child.
I use it to grow,
nourishment.
I am still growing.
I've renounced martyrdom.
I feel heat rippling,
emanating from my body.
This is where the crime was supposed to happen.
I've renounced the executioner's blade.
The recipient is not here to receive.
I shake my hands.
It does not affect another soul.

On April 28, 1986, Chernobyl Exploded

The news of the explosion sent us running into our homes.
We were not allowed to play outside for 10 days.
We were given medicine intravenously
and they purified the drinking water.

I ran around the living room
like a dog after its tail, after 3 days of confinement.
Mama read us stories to pass the time.
Nothing seemed to grab our attention.
We missed Tata.

We still do not know how this affects us now,
those of us so close to the explosion.
My ability to have children.

I recall the images on Russian TV
the site of the nuclear plant in Chernobyl,
not too far from Arad,
the burned building.
The smoke and soot that continued billowing
for days and days.

In my 20s, I became a Chemistry teacher in New York.
I taught my students about the table of elements.
Radon and Uranium did not stand out.
They radiated through me.

The Well

The East River is illuminated
and a dark bird darts into the sky from a tree.
You once lived in a peaceful treehouse.
Solitude is sometimes society.
I remember being in the womb
something about fluidity.
Being filled with fluid.

Was there a well in the back of the house?
Lia, the younger sister, told me she once fell into it.
My brother heard her screaming
and he pulled her out.
Did such a well exist?
Everything has a life of its own
and there is a house on the hill
lit from inside.
You love every floor,
no need to sweep.
The river is illuminated.
It is perfect.
Does not need anything.

Your bifid uvula hangs peacefully
as a fleshy extension in the back
of the soft palate.
And it moves.
The epiglottis flops open
while you breathe to allow air
into the larynx.

I smell of the outdoors,
my skin is windswept.
They never found Lia
at the bottom of the well.
You see, there never was a well
in the back of the house.

Notes on the Disappearances of Children

Was it autumn?
Were we visiting our friends in their small town?
Were the city planners dead?
A playground, outside the town cemetery.
The man approached us swiftly.
One cannot tell the head from the tail
of a snake in the tall grass.

The man was wearing a black trench coat.
The sky was a deep shade of gray.

He glided.
A ghost?

Run! The crow warned us.
We were swinging,
our heads high above the fence.
The graves and headstones,
let the man out of the woods.
He came for us.
What are children to do?
The crow warned against the approach
of the man.

No wind, yet the gate
keeps ringing.

Bloody Slide (Topogan)

At Dedi's butcher shop, after the slaughter of the animals, the meat makes its way down to the basement. The butchers clean and insert it through fireplace openings. The animals slide down to the room with the oversized scales. The butchers hang the slabs on ceiling hooks in the gigantic fridge. Sounds cannot be heard through the fridge doors, so this is where my brother and I play hide and seek. Screaming when we would find the other. In our school uniforms, we jumped through the opening onto the bloody slide and ended up on our bottoms in the weighing room. In our blood stained clothes, we leaped onto the large scales. The red needle pointed frantically right, both of us on the scale bouncing with laughter, until one of us would slide off the wet platform.

The Lamp

Under the lamp
rests my grandmother's
electrocuted body.
I have not seen her face,
smelled her hair,
nor felt the caress of her hands
in 20 years.

A wet cloth in her hand
an unprotected wire,
from the lamp and
the radiator;
closed circuit.

Why did she have to clean
the day before coming to America?
"Close your mouth you greedy child!
Don't cry out!"

It was August 1997.
In the heat
a plump body,
like the Romanian house
I dreamt of last night,
happy to return to my hometown of Arad.
I moved beside a younger
version of my father.
With him all worries perished.
A young version of my soul

singing at the thought
of a new beginning,
in an old country.

In the black and white photograph
I am two years old.
One hand is on the lamp.
I am turned away from the camera.

My grandmother's hair is already white.
She is looking at me,
knowing somehow
she would die twice.
Once when we left Romania
and once more
before we reunited.

The Plate

It flies,
white, round,
no longer
with the purpose
to serve or hold.

When it hits
it breaks
into pieces
that spread
sharp,
unrelenting,
unforgiving
like words.

How will our family
sit again,
eat from what is
left of the set,
without remembering
the broken sister?

The Oven

It had been a cold winter in Alba Iulia.
Aunt Gica and Uncle Traian,
were freezing in their bedroom.
She turned on the oven and opened
its door. This is how they fell asleep.

From the Gas Centrala,
someone cut the gas in the neighborhood overnight.
Too many people were using their ovens to stay warm.
The flames went out.

At 6 AM, the next morning
administrators in regulation gray
turned the gas back on at the Centrala.
The oven door was still open
in Gica's kitchen,
without the flame.

My aunt Gica was close to the door.
Her body lay there in rigor mortis.
One arm reaching up for the handle.
She could not open the door.
A week later they were found.
Later than death? They were.
And killed, they were.

Geographically Incorrect Justification for Torture

I shiver in my skin,
vomit the choked woman who
resides in the branches of my tendons,
calcifies a map of her residence with
this cylindrical ladder,
leads into the ministry of lost addresses,
dusty paintings of Jesus and Mary in the attic
of my grandparents' house,
(who later had to burn them for heat) –
descends into the chastity belt
where the vulva lost its rhythmical ticking.

On winter days in prison of white
crisp bed sheets and square feather pillows,
my head,
disinfected of lice
beats to the drum of the slaughtered pig,
his blood gushes as if through my belly button.
His throat cut with the boat carving knife.

I bounce at each garish shriek,
Milk myself of the peaceful white
Till I am decalcified and blue
In the guilty cheek,
House of adulterous lips
Of father and grandfather.

Operatic concert going on in the yard,
battlefield for blades of grass who want
to soak up water, not blood.
The hourglass stops flowing
as my period does when the inflamed
braided veins of my uterus
listen to the nonexistent
body for sale.

I am parked in the doorway,
where two tin cans hold
tails, ears, livers draining for goulash,
feet waiting to be soaked in garlic juice
and frozen, when November will come.

Esophagus inside esophagus
breathing anti-rhythmically to create
sensations of entitlement.
We even ate the throats.
sometimes the glassy eyes,
the ears, the tails,
all that brought the neighborhood together
was the butcher,
my grandfather.

Afraid of nature,
of the nature of all lights out,
during Christmas,
during homework nights,
black and white American films,
during the abortion.
All lights out.

Bundás Kenyér

You are cooking Bundás Kenyér,
my sweet Dedi, down the hall
in the kitchen. My body is under
the down comforter.
My childhood face floats above fever.
The smell that brings it all back. I have
cooked, fried, and cut meats
like you, dear Dedi. When I opened
the door, the scent of my imaginary
clementine was stopped dead in its tracks.
Nothing, I tell you, nothing works like
Bundás Kenyér to return me
to a sudden forgotten memory.
I go around naming things.
Dedi=Grandfather. Bundás Kenyér=French Toast.
It is the elusiveness of the smell that make
a little dream of me. I want to stay
here with my childhood face, my fever,
covered in the heaviness of the comforter,
waiting impatiently to take a first bite.

Hunger

You have to sacrifice yourself for your family.
You become fat.
You are fat and sacrificial like a lamb.
They eat lamb and other meat for Easter.
They forget to demand of you your skin
along with your organs.
Your mind.
They are territorial nonetheless.
You have to be the black sheep.
They stuff their faces and choke on the bones.
Never again will they use the same butcher for Easter.

For Mihai Eminescu

Eminescu este chipul infinitului din noi. —*Adrian Paunescu*

Eminescu mi-e dor de tine.
Eminescu, I miss you.
Your face is the infinite in all of us.
Re-assorted and disassembled
I tried to glue you back, dear Eminescu
on the lapel of my heart.
I listen to those reciting your poems in Romanian.
Those who ring my phone at night
and sing verses from Luceafarul.
You are looking down at me.
At the poet that I am.
You are waiting.
But this is not the truth.
I miss the land of cherry trees and plum trees.
We sat in the orchards and ate the fruit.
Some fell to the ground and we picked them up,
lifted them to our lips.
The rose petals in clusters on the grass.
It was nearing September.

Russian Connection

for Anna Akmatova

Dad's words,
then muffled snores,
cut the thread of poetry,
hers and mine;
leaving behind a dotted line,
black minuses and shadows
on white sheets of forgiveness.

Crumbs in the Forest

1. Garden

I have a garden of my own for 13 years. I tend to it. We never
see the beginning and the end of anything. The stitched yellow
numbers on my uniform sleeve, everpresent. To the wolves!
They devour the numbers. Our German Shepherd, Nero is
feasting. The bowl from which he eats is not broken. The art of
precious scars. I take my friend to the attic. My head you break
by throwing a brick. Golden joinery and repair work. My index
finger slips into the hole in my forehead then the blood starts
gushing. This is what I know of broken bones. It is not the only
bone I ever break.

2. One of my Own

As a baby I slip through my mother's fingers when she falls asleep.
Why did she let me go? It is the one thing I do not do with Luna,
my niece. I do not fall asleep. As long as I have her in my arms.
My lower back is in such pain, yet I hold on. My index finger is
in her left hand. As she falls asleep, the grip loosens and her hand
suddenly lets go. In the middle of the night, I stand with her in
my arms and I rock her to sleep.

3. Mercy

Ceausescu, Romania's former Dictator, is a man limited by logic.
He imprisons the people whose thinking is infinite. I lose myself
for a moment, a year, maybe twenty. I push beyond the limit
of my conscience into the substrata of the subconscious mind.
The levels push back, as I descend. I am what I appear to be.
Hallucinating. Displaced. Disassociated from my body. Post
traumatic and… so many posts… that I cannot count. But, let
me count the ways. I dropped the crumbs in the forest. Why did
you not come? I have gotten eaten by the wolves and spit out by
coyotes. Here I am. I stand. In front of you.

4. Family

I do not imagine that my first 13 years of life in Romania are
a holding station. Surrendering in translation is a form of
persecution. The autodidact can easily love self-flagellation.
Raised in Romanian, what do I remember? After I forget my
language, I remember: *cadou, dor, durere.* Gift. Longing. Pain.
I am dipped in their DNA pool. *Mama si tata. Buni si dedi.*
Buni si mosu. Two parents. Four grandparents. Sixteen great
grandparents. I do not capitalize on forgetting. I play with
memory. I rearrange it in your bullshit language. Laugh at a few
jokes. Understand very few stories. Some people. I collect their
reflections and discard them later. I am cold. I have no country.
No language. No loyalty. I remember: *revedere, peron, tren,*
farmec, presimtire, iubire si sfarsit.

5. The Gold Foil Experiment

The narrow beam of light broadens when it passes through a
thin film of mica. The particles move quickly. Expectations.
Scattering. Small. Radioactive. Particles emitted are small.
Electric and magnetic fields. A figurina spotted dancing across
the gold. How science got women wrong. Our chemistry.
Our fabric. Our DNA. Start working on it now. Mend things.
Understand by offering to listen. Lean into it. We say what we
feel, sometimes. Be the whistleblower. Approach it from our
angle. Even bones are continually maintained.

6. Melody for a Funeral

I am standing in front of the firing squad. My soul extends like
my own hands, receiving sounds. Charging their weapons. It
comes in waves. First, buried memories, dreams, struggles, my
own detering present, despair and then, nothing. The symphony
ends with utter insistence on silence. We are facing each other. I
know you kill. I know you will kill. I know. My crime? My

anguished harmony with light. I see all of it. I begin to feel my despair turn into beauty. This is how you kill me. In my ecstasy. With nothing on my lips.

We Pass Through History

The spider signifies "news is coming",
and it crawls on me during the night
bites my eye, causing the inflamed eyelid
to swell into a perfect cupola.

Our resolve is to belong to ourselves,
beget coffee beans, a priest,
round, wire rimmed glasses,
and an open window.
Debunk the superstitions
of our youth.
Wear charcoal on our eyes.
See into others' souls.

We pass through history as bleeding angels.
Rationed milk makes our children starve,
we all starve. Mother's breasts are not lactating.
Rationed bread, meat, oil,
sugar and butter.
The thinnest slices of salami, tomatoes
and Feta cheese on our plates.

Crows hover on the fence
of those who die within a week.
Our friends and neighbors disappear.
We seek angels our entire lives.
"ADELAAAAAA. Come out to play."
Children call out while we eat slabs of meat.
Our teeth fall out of our adult mouths.

Walking on the streets of New York City,
years later, the street looks to be carpeted
with gemstones.
Scattered, sharp, unrelenting
in their shine.

Romanian poet watches new installment of Unsolved Mysteries Episode 1

All it takes is an empty street.
This is what I fear most.
Not the ghosts, demons, nor angels
I saw at the age of 23.

>They taught us in school: everyone must do their jobs.
>The way entities overtook me.
>After all, even our teachers.
>Brainwashing can last a lifetime.
>Before the garbage cleaners
>will dispose of the trash.

All it takes is an empty street.
Were there any witnesses
at the Belvedere Hotel
in the middle of that night?
His body dropped
through the ceiling
into the conference room.
An accident? How was it
geographically possible?
His bones shattered.
The courtyard was empty.

I am afraid of what they will find.
Everyone who saw it shuts their mouths.
I am afraid stamina means
staying where you are not wanted.
The ones who are vindictive
do it in ways you cannot imagine.

>All it takes is an empty street.
>I am at the window looking out.
>Mother, you've told me one too many
>secrets.

Your words are the window.
You are the window.
I shatter with understanding.

So what if I smelled the blood first?
We are all born bloodied.
Isn't there enough liquid
for the world to get wet?
What wants out must be birthed.
Sometimes bridled.

Holding the sparrow in my hands
the words flush out.
A mural of headlines, confessions and verdicts.
You've told me one too many secrets.

The witnesses at the Belvedere
all followed the same script.
They lied with authority and conviction.
Nobody saw his body fall
nor be pushed
off the roof of the hotel.
The hole in the ceiling
his body fell through
still there.
Gravity was faster than him
he could have changed his mind
on the way down
falling,
falling deep under.

Kitchen Objects

The table, covered in a checkered red and white linoleum tablecloth, is smack in the middle of the kitchen. The plates, cups, glasses, pot and pans, are piled up in the cupboard, ready for the concert. The long knives hang on nails inside the green cabinet to the left of the cupboard. They are ready to cling, cling, cling and rattle metal to metal in their own sharp, unrelenting ways. Menacing the other spectators, who at most can be bruised, pushed off the shelves and break into shards on the floor. Who knows if they ever will? The shaking just won't stop. The beginning of an earthquake that sends trembles through all atoms. Everything that goes together, like the four chairs under the table, begins separating. A child loses the grip of their mom's hand in a large crowd in the public square. This kind of rupture. The undeniably irreparable kind.

Are the spectators giving the concert? Then, who is even listening? Is the house tilting to one side? The floorboards are at a slant, the cupboard is lopsided. How can we keep it all level? We must push through the narrative to the other side. The plates, cups, glasses and pans are not enough. Not even the menacing knives. Not enough. Introduce some characters… How long can a reader peruse about inanimate objects?

Here comes the son. He is 8 years old. As soon as he enters the kitchen, he pulls out a chair and sits to face the cupboard and the green cabinet. His face tilted to one side, expectant. Nothing on his plate. Where is his father? When will his mother be home? Shards of glass are spread on the uneven floor. How is he going to explain this to his parents? The shrills of the knives took over the kitchen quiet hour. Will the wrinkles in the middle of his forehead show his surprise? Will they forgive him? Or does he seem older now amidst destruction. Like a war survivor, a child amidst the rubble. His town is not spared the Cold War, but somehow opera and classical music survive. When the plates fall the music on the radio starts accompanying the opera in the kitchen. All is covered in shards, blue and white, like the foaming sea. The boy is immobile and does not know how he will break away from this scene. For he is barefoot. The floors are cold and uninviting to his bare feet. He feels a chill rush from the bottom of his feet, up his spine, to the top of his head. The air hissed. The kitchen waited. The son waited. For his sister.

Crepes

I searched with desperation and a salivating mouth for a crepe recipe. I called mama first. She quickly responded that she did not remember the proportions and the quantities. Then, I called my step-mother, who was driving to Publix to pick up some eggs for breakfast. She rushed me off the phone, since she could not remember the ratio of eggs to flour. But she did say: "I use seltzer in mine instead of milk!"

I then reached out to Cristina, whose mother always said to add a few drops of oil into the mix. That was her contribution to my morning recipe. Raluca, my cousin from Romania, googled the recipe and texted it to me. I finally had the steps!

So from one mother to another mother, I traversed the land of crepes. I cracked 2 eggs open in a large bowl, added 300 grams of flour, then 250 milliliters of milk, slowly and then finally the pinch of salt and a few drops of oil. My pan was hot and the oil rippled in it. The ladle was filled to the top with the mixture. I baked the first one and the sweet aroma filled me like no mother could. Not mama, not my step-mother, not Cristina's mother, nor Raluca.

Over the burning pan I became my own mother. I had to cross the Atlantic Ocean, climb mountains like the Carpathians, the Adirondacks and the Catskills, to arrive here and look down at my creation.

With Special Thanks

With special thanks to Michael F. Goldburg for his love and devotion. I also would like to thank Holly Wren Spaulding for editing the early manuscript and for her beautiful endorsement for my book. Much gratitude to Cristina A. Bejan who is and always will be a great inspiration.

Cover description—the pictures appearing on the cover of the book are of Sinclair's family members, grandmothers, grandfather, father, mother, her brother and cousin. All the objects depicted on the cover are Sinclair's possessions, her fountain pens, the crochet pieces her grandmother made and the postcard her best friend Lavinia wrote to her.

Romanian translation of terms from poems in
La Revedere (Goodbye):

La revedere—goodbye, with the hope of meeting again
Buni—grandmother
Dedi—grandfather
Tata—father
Alimnetara—grocery story
peron—train platform
tren—train
farmec—charm
presimtire—premonition
iubire—love
sfarsit—end

Adela Sinclair is a Romanian-American poet, translator, and teacher. Fluent in English, French, and Romanian, poetry is her primary, though not exclusive, medium. She is inspired by the Romanian poets and intellectuals of the '70s and '80s, such as Nina Cassian, Ana Blandiana, Nichita Stanescu, Tristan Tzara, and Paul Celan. Her poetry explores themes of cultural identity, memory, loss, trauma, and desire. Her work appears on *The Bridge*, published by Brooklyn Poets, and Tupelo Press' *30/30 Project*. Adela is currently working with an editor on her first full-length poetry collection, *The Butcher's Granddaughter*, a lyrical memoir of her childhood in Romania. She has performed her poetry all over New York City including the Yale Club, 92nd Street Y, Bowery Poetry Club, Poet's House, Brooklyn Poets, Books are Magic, KGB Bar, Saint Francis College, and Writer's Voice at the JCC. She is a founding member and poetry editor of the emerging literary magazine, *Unbound Brooklyn*, and volunteers with Ugly Duckling Presse in Brooklyn.

Adela was a poet-in-residence at Gallery RIVAA, a New York City art gallery, where she led poetry workshops. She also worked as their Events Director and Special Promotions Curator, where she hosted book readings for *Unorthodox* by Deborah Feldman, *The Luminist* by David Rocklin, *Echo Train* by Aaron Fagan, and several book launches for Nina Cassian, a trusted confidante, mentor, friend and beloved neighbor for more than ten years. Adela produced/co-hosted the radio show "Notebook Writer" on Blog Talk Radio where she interviewed such writers as Amy Tan, author of *The Joy Luck Club*. She has 20 years of experience as a teacher in the New York City public and private school systems. As a writing teacher at The École, an independent, French-American bilingual school, Adela led groups of elementary and middle school students to share their original poems, in French and English, for four years at the annual "Poem in Your Pocket Day" in the Bryant Park Reading Room during National Poetry Month.

Adela is a member and supporter of Poetry Forge, Writers Without Borders, Poet's House, Pen America, Author's Guild, Poetry Society of America, and Poetry Society of New York. Her teachers and mentors include such luminaries as Annie Finch, Sharon Olds, Ariana Reines, Reggie Cabbico, Marlon James, Mahogany Brown, Rachel Zucker, Brenda Hillman, Nathalie Handal, and Hermine Meinhard. Adela holds a BA in French Culture and Civilization from SUNY Albany, with additional coursework at the Sorbonne University of Paris, an MA in Education from Hunter College (NYC), and an MFA in Creative Writing/Poetry from St. Francis College (Brooklyn). A Reiki Master, she also offers private healing sessions. In a prior life, Adela managed two Indie Rock bands, The Apartment Years and Via Wireless, and produced the music video "Ativan Day" for Via Wireless. She lives in New York City.

www.ingramcontent.com/pod-product-compliance
Lightning Source LLC
Chambersburg PA
CBHW030459100426
42813CB00002B/278